NOTE TO PARENTS

Learning to read is an important skill for all children. It is a big milestone that you can help your child reach. The American Museum of Natural History Easy Reader program is designed to support you and your child through this process. Developed by reading specialists, each book in the series includes carefully selected words and sentence structures to help children advance from beginner to intermediate to proficient readers.

Here are some tips to keep in mind as you read these books with your child:

First, preview the book together. Read the title. Then look at the cover. Ask your child, "What is happening on the cover? What do you think this book is about?"

Next, skim through the pages of the book and look at the illustrations. This will help your child use the illustrations to understand the story.

Then encourage your child to read. If he or she stumbles over words, try some of these strategies:

- **use the pictures as clues**
- **point out words that are repeated**
- **sound out difficult words**
- **break up bigger words into smaller chunks**
- **use the context to lend meaning**

Finally, find out if your child understands what he or she is reading. After you have finished reading, ask, "What happened in this book?"

Above all, understand that each child learns to read at a different rate. Make sure to praise your young reader and provide encouragement along the way!

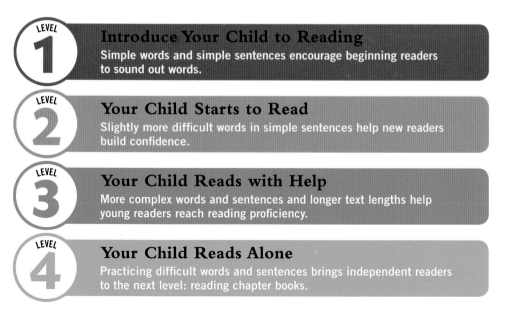

LEVEL 1

Introduce Your Child to Reading
Simple words and simple sentences encourage beginning readers to sound out words.

LEVEL 2

Your Child Starts to Read
Slightly more difficult words in simple sentences help new readers build confidence.

LEVEL 3

Your Child Reads with Help
More complex words and sentences and longer text lengths help young readers reach reading proficiency.

LEVEL 4

Your Child Reads Alone
Practicing difficult words and sentences brings independent readers to the next level: reading chapter books.

For Vida, who likes to scram around the house at top speed.
—M.S.

Photo credits
Cover/jacket/title page: © Martin Harvey/Alamy
4–5: © Mc Donald Wildlife Photo/Animals Animals; 6–7: © Villiers Steyn/Shutterstock;
8–9: ©Pictureguy66/Dreamstime; 10–11: © NaluPhoto/iStockphoto; 12–13: © Andrea Izzotti/Shutterstock;
14–15: © Jeff Vanuga/Corbis; 16: © sergey23/Shutterstock; 17: © NHPA/SuperStock;
18–19: © Kajornyot/Dreamstime; 20–21: © Images of Africa Photobank/Alamy; 22–23: © Frans Lanting/Corbis;
24–25: © MonicaOttino/Shutterstock; 26–27: © Emory Kristof/National Geographic Stock;
28–29: © DEA Picture Library/age fotostock; 30-31: © WaterFrame/Alamy;
32: © Chris Raxworthy

STERLING CHILDREN'S BOOKS
New York

An Imprint of Sterling Publishing
387 Park Avenue South
New York, NY 10016

ISBN 978-1-4549-0633-9 (hardcover)
ISBN 978-1-4027-7793-6 (paperback)

Distributed in Canada by Sterling Publishing
c/o Canadian Manda Group, 165 Dufferin Street
Toronto, Ontario, Canada M6K 3H6
Distributed in the United Kingdom by GMC Distribution Services
Castle Place, 166 High Street, Lewes, East Sussex, England BN7 1XU
Distributed in Australia by Capricorn Link (Australia) Pty. Ltd.
P.O. Box 704, Windsor, NSW 2756, Australia

For information about custom editions, special sales, and premium and corporate purchases,
please contact Sterling Special Sales at 800-805-5489 or specialsales@sterlingpublishing.com.

Printed in China
Lot #:
2 4 6 8 10 9 7 5 3 1
01/14

www.sterlingpublishing.com/kids

FREE ACTIVITIES & PUZZLES ONLINE AT
http://www.sterlingpublishing.com/kids/sterlingeventkits

AMERICAN MUSEUM
OF NATURAL HISTORY

EASY READERS

World's Fastest Animals

Melissa Stewart

STERLING CHILDREN'S BOOKS
New York

Can you run on top of water?

No way!

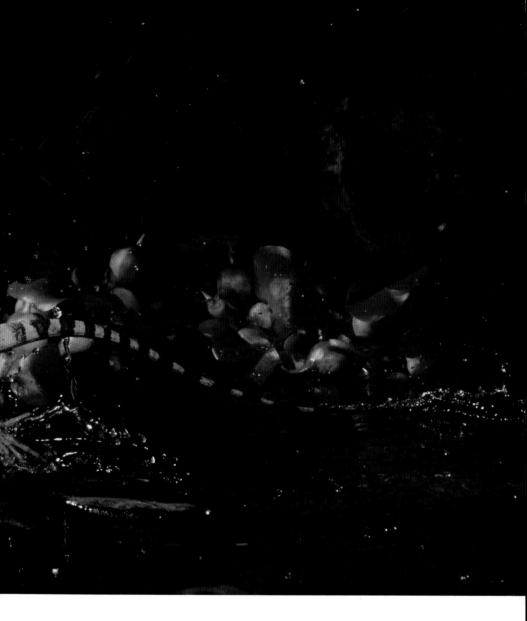

A basilisk lizard can.

It darts across water so fast that it does not sink in.

Let's meet some other fast animals!

A cheetah is the fastest animal

on land.

It can run 64 miles per hour.

But a cheetah cannot run fast

for long.

It must slow down after about

20 seconds.

A pronghorn antelope cannot run as
fast as a cheetah.

Its top speed is 53 miles per hour.

But the antelope can run fast for
miles and miles.

No other animal can run as far
at top speed.

Some fish are even faster than
a cheetah.

A sailfish can swim up to 68 miles
per hour.

Its super speed helps it catch smaller fish to eat.

The sailfish is the fastest swimmer in the world.

Look at this peregrine falcon flying!

It is diving for food.

This falcon is the fastest animal alive.

It can dive at a speed of more than

200 miles per hour.

An ostrich is a bird that cannot fly.

But look at it run!

It races across grasslands at 43

miles per hour.

An ostrich is the fastest animal
on two legs.

A honey bee's wings whiz through
the air.

Its wings beat 200 times a second!

The wings on gnats are even faster.

A gnat's wings beat 1,000 times
per second!

Gnats have the fastest wings in the world.

Some animals run. Others swim or fly.

But gibbons swing from tree to tree.

Look at this gibbon's long arms and

big hands.

They help it swing through the forest
at 35 miles per hour.

No other animal can swing that fast.

Most of the time an aardvark is slow.

But this animal is fast when it comes

to digging.

One aardvark can dig a tunnel faster than a team of people with shovels.

Look at this chameleon's tongue!

It is twice as long as its body.

The chameleon has the fastest tongue on Earth.

It can grab an insect faster than you can blink your eyes.

Can you feel your heart beating?

A child's heart pumps blood 80 to 100

times a minute.

A hummingbird has the fastest heart on Earth.

How fast does its heart beat?

It beats up to 1,200 times a minute. Wow!

Take a look at these giant tubeworms.

They live deep in the ocean.

They can grow three feet long in one year.

That sure is fast!

Snails are some of the slowest
animals on Earth.

So why is a snail in this book?

This cone snail can catch fish very fast.

Do you see what is sticking out
of its shell? It looks like a tongue.
That "tongue" shoots poison into fish
at top speed.

A mantis shrimp has fast claws.

Its claws can punch up to 50 miles

per hour. The punch breaks open

a clam's hard shell.

Then the shrimp eats the clam's soft body.

Being fast helps all kinds of animals survive in the world.

MEET THE EXPERT!

I am **Chris Raxworthy**, a herpetologist at the American Museum of Natural History. A herpetologist studies modern species of amphibians and reptiles. As a young boy I loved catching salamanders and frogs, and I still remember the first time I held a python; it was at a zoo when I was four. My pet tortoise, Persephone, still lives with me. I bought her in a pet shop in 1979. While I was at university in London, England, I studied zoology and learned about many fast animals, like the ones you've just read about. Working at the American Museum of Natural History means I am always learning new and exciting things about our natural world.

My research includes exploring little-known tropical forests in Madagascar, Africa, and in the Indian Ocean. I look for new species of reptiles and amphibians, and I describe where and how to find them. Sometimes we walk for several days to reach a study area. My favorite reptiles are chameleons. More than half the world's species of chameleons are found only in Madagascar.

When I am back at the Museum, I use my field results, the research collections, and our laboratories to look at the form, genetics, and geographic locations of the animals I study. This helps us to protect rare species and better understand how these species evolved and what habitats they need. I also teach students, work on exhibitions, such as our exhibition *Frogs: A Chorus of Colors*, and help make all kinds of books, including this one!